KEEPING IT REAL III
"THE OTHER SIDE OF THE VEIL"

VerShay "DominaRex" DuVall

authorHOUSE®

AuthorHouse™
1663 Liberty Drive
Bloomington, IN 47403
www.authorhouse.com
Phone: 1 (800) 839-8640

Published by AuthorHouse 03/09/2015

ISBN: 978-1-4969-7476-1 (sc)
ISBN: 978-1-4969-7475-4 (e)

Print information available on the last page.

This book is printed on acid-free paper.

KJV
Scripture quotations marked KJV are from the Holy Bible, King James Version (Authorized Version). First published in 1611. Quoted from the KJV Classic Reference Bible, Copyright © *1983 by The <u>Zondervan</u> Corporation.*

DEDICATION

*T*his book is dedicated to all those who have suffered adverse consequences in and out of the church. I dedicate this book to those that feared telling their testimony for fear of being ridiculed by their peers and loved ones. I dedicate this book to those that have suffered from mental illness and/or lost a loved one to suicide because of the pressures of ministry and the sin they may have been too embarrassed to seek prayer for.

I truly thank my Lord and Savior Jesus Christ for giving me a village of family and friends assigned specifically to my life. I am truly a walking testimony of deliverance, healing and freedom from bondage and strongholds.

The Lord intended for the Christian Community to know that the Body of Christ can only be built on the truth, and that there is no room for falsehoods if you believe in the Holy Bible. I speak life and light into the dark places of the lives of leaders and lay members. Please recognize that we have to come to terms with all sin in our lives in order to be effective in ministry, love and life.

To my village.....the truth will make you free, so come on over to the other side of the veil!

CONTENTS

HER STORY (1)

*M*en and Women of God I come to you in all humility. I have been in my tenth (10th) season for a few years now. This season consists of my Testimony and The law of Responsibility. This is a crucial stage of my spiritual maturity and the anointing God has placed on my life, and the mantle's in which I am responsible to carry. My story is my past from a child to an adult that suffered from trauma, drama and manipulated man-made chaos and confusion; and not to mention recovering from mental illness. This story is mine; and the boat I was in was mine; and the healing and deliverance is mine to hold onto as a permanent miracle. The Lord had me sit for a little over ten (10) years, and in this time frame I was able to see my mistakes, made more mistakes, but learned throughout the process, learned to rely on God; submit to the processes; and be equipped for the new journey I was going to take. I had to realize that settling for less than what God made me into was the enemies trick to keep me bound, and that it was learned behavior. Ah....Yes, I have a wonderful educational history, and the earned degrees to substantiate my legitimacy, but it didn't stop me from experiencing the wickedness that so easily befalls us in life, love and ministry. I hope while reading this book, you will begin to experience the love of Christ and know that we all have to answer to God for our public and private iniquities. I am glad that mine were exposed prior to His making me into a completely restored, reconciled, recovered, regenerated and refined woman of God approved as a vessel to be used by Him.

We have to recognize that when we keep secrets, it hurts us more than anything. The hard part is recovering when you have built yourself up, and then want others to worship you instead of Our Heavenly Father.

We preach and teach our members in our respective congregations regardless of how large or small they are to seek His face, but do we? We preach and teach the people who are still babes in Christ to listen to what thus said the Lord, and all the while it is us, the leaders who need the presence of the Holy Spirit. We want the anointing so bad that we manufacture it, we act out what we know it looks like, we stage the effects and emotionalize ourselves and others into yearning for that experience; and enter in only to find out that it was about self, emotion and money. Don't get me wrong, money keeps the ministry running, not your house, your car, your clothes and everything else associated with what money can buy. But when money starts to supersede the Word of God, the enemy has done his job to distort and pervert God, and you.

You see I no longer have anything to lose; because I lost everything that I built a little over 10 years ago. It is now time to get what God would want me to have. I am now released to speak the truth into the lives of others without sin knocking at my door and throwing it up in my face as a shadow of the past telling me who I used to be, and what I'm not going to ever be. I am now released to continue ministry in the true Name of Jesus Christ! I am now released to let the world know about me and how I made it to the other side of the veil.

Had I not went through the storms, pain, mistakes, hurt and the breaking, I might not have fallen in love with Jesus all over again. Because "secrets kill," I can speak out of my own experience, my healing, my deliverance and freedom from strongholds and bondage. I can now speak to giants that disrupt the lives of others, and lead them through a process that can set them free. I can now say "stop hiding behind the spotlights of what it looks like" and present yourselves as a living sacrifice.

We have been taught to go along, to get along, and its time to open up a Pandora's box in your life and start a controversy with yourself as I did. If the truth be told, church hurt causes a lot of issues, but knowing who you are in Christ will allow you to digest the isms and schisms that come along with the territory. We think we are exempt from the issues of life, but in fact we as leaders are ministering from a broken place and closets of secrets, shame and iniquity. We fall short like anyone else, and God holds us more accountable for the souls entrusted to us to shepherd, equip, and train and disciple. We strive to get to the Kingdom of God, and hope He has mercy on us on the way, and forgiveness that pardoned our rebellious sin sick selves. God is requiring that the bar be raised and the truth step to the plate. I couldn't have re-written my testimony if God wasn't requiring me to be responsible as a soul care-giver. I can compare myself to so many people in the Bible, and identify with scenarios, set-ups, hook-ups, and more; but this is my story; and you haven't heard it before, but you may relate.

So please don't look for the highly educated woman of God to speak as an intellectual in this edition. Try to see, hear and feel where I'm coming from. My heart was heavy on this journey of being under construction and reclaiming my dignity, my character, my integrity, and my birth rights as a child of the King. Travel with me as I journey to the side of the veil, and into a new season of greatness and abundant freedom into the next dimension and realm of God's mandate on my life.

KEEPING IT REAL (2)

But now, O Lord, thou art our father; we are the clay and thou
our potter; and we all are the work of thy hand - Isaiah 64:8

I am truly thankful for this passage of scripture. I had to meditate on this for yet a while before the Holy Spirit woke me up out of my sleep to begin to write this book. I have wrestled with the start of this book for quite sometime. As we all do, but I will only speak for myself when I say I procrastinated. I am keeping this real because the world I live in is real, but my reality is to see the Kingdom of God.

I can reflect on how I hid behind so many things in life that caused me stress, depression, sin, lust, etc. Broken by the things of this world that I was not exempt from. I found myself trapped in despair, not knowing which way to turn or who to turn to. I knew the Lord was on my side all the time, but when was I as an anointed and appointed woman of God going to realize that God too keeps it real!

When was I going to realize that His word, is His word, and He doesn't change it up!

Me, the Archbishop had to report to the most High and get a clear direction from Him? Why was I thinking because I had it all wrapped up and tied up in the Holy Ghost that it didn't make me exempt in my weakest hour! Who did I think I was walking around perpetrating to feel ok when inside I was torn, broke down and disgusted about my life and everything in it. I was angry, I was bitter, I was evil, and I was flat out sinful! Everything Jesus stood for; I was on the road to hell with no way back. Not keeping it real almost cost me my life, my children, my family, my friends and my ministry.

How many of us in ministry have ever felt like this? I mean when do we keep it real and tell the people the truth about ourselves. I was broken! I had a nervous breakdown! I forgot I had a potter! I forgot I had a maker! I forgot for a short while who He (GOD) called me to be! The clay form didn't exist anymore. I was unstoppable, unshakeable, and unmovable. I had an attitude of how dare you!

Yes, little ole' me Archbishop had the potter and the clay twisted, and GOD had to reminded me, so I sought His help!

I needed some intervention. I had to be like Isaiah and plead for God to come down and intervene in my private nation, and in my private affairs. I know that Isaiah asked God to come and help the nations. God's presence was described as a melting fire that would make the nations tremble. Well, my nation trembled crumbled, sagged, lagged and melted away. I was left with nothing. The world that I set up had covered up issues like: mental illness, lies, a homosexual experience, lust, lack of, depression, anger, hurt, pain, anguish, misunderstood, loneliness, past fears, doubts, rape, molestation, drug abuse, alcohol abuse, divorce, domestic violence, not to mention being saved and other ministers preying on you.

I know the great prophet of God yet realized that we are all unclean (*tame*, this is a technical term for legal impurity). *All our righteousness are as filthy rags*. I was the depravity of mankind. I was in this condition of sinful depravity; *there is none that calleth upon thy name.* Isaiah pleaded with not to judge *thy people* but to extend *mercy.*

This was me people of God. I needed an Isaiah to plead my case. I couldn't plead for myself. I was too far gone. I was out of control. I just knew I was doing everything right! I had trust issues and it's not to say I still don't, but my reality is that the hurt had been too deep to release, and I couldn't go to just anybody anymore. All our righteousness is as filthy rags; and I was stinking at this point and couldn't stand myself. I don't care how many baths, showers, perfume, powder perfume, all of that still didn't cover up the stench that I represented as a woman, a mother, sister, daughter or leader in the community, and as a representative of being one of God's chosen vessels hand made by Him.

Life threw me a curve ball. I cried and cried because the house that God had given me had been consumed with fire and burned up. His presence made me tremble with fear, and that's when I knew my foolishness was over. I had to submit to the Father and accept the circumstances that came with the submission. God made me realize that He made me for this appointed hour to lead His people, and that all that I have been through, He allowed. At that point I felt like Job, but still didn't understand why me? I have the schools, I have the ministries, I have the skill, and I have this great status all over the world…Ah… I, I, I., this was the problem! I stopped giving God the praise for what He had done for me; He needed me to be broken; He broke me in such a way that I couldn't call on anyone but Him. I mean momma, daddy, girlfriends, so-called friends, ministry folks, none of which could pray for me. I had become lost in a pool of water that needed to be stirred up by an angel sent from above. My mind checked out on me.

In my transparency, I was over rebellious at this point. I had to go back and find out who I really was. Yes I had Christ in my heart; yes I confessed my sins for myself; yes I know who Jesus is; yes I accepted and had a relationship with Jesus at an early age, but know I had to find out what went wrong; what was the cause of this rebellion at this point in my life? So I had to believe that God was going to bring a seed out of Jacob; I believed as Paul insisted that God has not forsaken His people Israel. So I began to focus on the Plain of Sharon and the valley of Achor. I was going to blossom abundantly and look forward to the prosperity of spiritual maturity, and if He did it for Israel during the millennial kingdom, I know He's going to do it for me personally, and restore me!

Whew....I began to repent. I didn't need to be in a church building physically. My home became my church! The coffee table, the couch, my bedside, the kitchen table, the stairs, the banister, the tub, the sink, the dining room table, the car, the store. There were a lot of places that became my repentance, worship, prayer, altar, and praise times; you name it, I broke down and gave God thanks for what He had healed, delivered and released me from in advance, so the strongholds and bondage could be snatched away.

As the prophet Isaiah begins to speak about the new heavens and a new earth in *Revelation 21.* I too was thrust into the celestial future to see the New Jerusalem, knowing that weeping and crying shall be no more *Revelation 21:4*; "And *God shall wipe away all tears from their eyes; and there shall be no more death, neither sorrow, nor crying, neither shall there be any more pain: for the former things are passed away. V5 And he that sat upon the throne said, Behold, I make all things new. And he said unto me, Write; for these words are true and faithful. V6 And he said unto me, It is done. I am Alpha and Omega, the beginning and the end. I will give unto him that is athirst of the fountain of water of life freely.*

Hallelujah…I now understood the passage of being the clay and being molded for His (God's) purpose and not mine. Glory…I respect the reality of my story in hopes that others in ministry can keep it real with the people of God whom they serve. God said it is done! All the things I went through have been accomplished for a purpose, and now its time to move on, and let it go! I have become part of His Holy purpose to gather a holy, devoted people for Him.

He let me know through the prophet that *Alpha and Omega* was my focus; *Beginning:* God was the source of all things; *End* He is also the goal of all things that I should be aiming for. He let me know that I have a right, and that He is available 24/7, 365 days a year for me.

Men and women alike, I know that I was dying spiritually, because of sin. My rebellion and weakness at this particular time in my life was a build up issues I never dealt with as a child, teenager and young adult. Keeping it real and speaking the truth was going to be the only way I was going to escape the hands of the enemy and the life-style of sin I so willingly chose based on what I was reared around, and having kept mentality.

I had to claim and declare for real that I refused to be released out of my relationship, fellowship, worship, and praise that would hinder me from inheriting the Kingdom of God on Earth, and forfeit my right to get to through the Kingdom of Heaven on earth and focus on the Kingdom of God, and transitioning my state of mind to a Kingdom state of mind that works in the supernatural realm seeing beyond what man comprehends as living.

Automatic Grace (3)

S inging "I got Five (5) on it." This number represents God's Grace for me. I was in need of a blessing, and it wasn't financial, or material. It was knowing that I still had a relationship with the Almighty. I was lost and could not be found by mankind. I mean people tried to pray, but because of their own iniquity, they couldn't get a prayer through.

People put me down, talked about me, and disrespected me, but never to my face. The ones who were supposed to be in my corner as mentioned before; so-called friends who were intercessors, well, they left me too! God began again to let me know that the only power that was going to be strong enough to pick me up was His. The Anointing from the Holy Spirit within my soul was going to need to be revived in such a way that mankind would and could not understand

My Grace period had started. I took a step back from ministry; I took a step back from people; I took a step back from teaching: I actually took a step back from the world at large and began where I started from; the beginning, with me. God began to purge those things that were not like Christ. It wasn't meant for me to be around hundreds of people to watch me be restored. They, the people in the Body of Christ already had no power, and the ones that were anointed had no anointing to deliver me. I needed a spiritual renewal that would take a covering so powerful that no one could have me join or fellowship with.

Wow! Back to the Anointed One who is the lover of my soul. I had gotten back to my first love Jesus Christ! I mean when I submitted and poured out my soul verbally, the love and power of God filled the house like never before. When I say house, I mean me. I could not contain what was being poured in. My windows of my soul began to bulge; the hurt, pain, anger, homosexuality, anger, lack of, domestic violence, rape, molestation, incest, and mental illness was being purged! You see some things were gone and never to return, but in order for the Grace (5) to kick in, I had to get rid of this stuff in order for Him (God) to have His famous twins of Grace and Mercy, on me.

As I preached and taught I knew I had to come out and tell the world about what kind of God I serve. The only one who can really heal you from a sin sick world of fleshly addictions and afflictions that you may or may not have willingly played a part in.

When I began to look back over my life and reviewed all that has ever happen to me, I should be in an institution locked up or dead. The average Christian or just human being probably would've taken their own life by now. I said God has been keeping a secret from me until now; because I am not average; I am very peculiar!

I have been being prepared (*hetoimazo*) for a divine purpose, it had been set-up for me before the foundation of this earth. In my mother's womb, the Lord knew of my downfalls. He knew I was going to fall short. He knew a hit, a contract had been put out on me by Satan, and he was going to and fro seeking me in order to devour that which God has called and chosen me to be. Wow….I can write a whole lot of fancy words that would move the average scholar, or intellectual being, but Grace from God is a five (5) letter word that doesn't need to be expounded upon. It stands alone.

I thought I had *"Automatic Grace."* Who was I kidding just because I was in ministry? I was accountable for all the lives I spoke into. I was going to have to pay the price for anyone who followed me and fell short because I falsely divided the wrong Word of God. First, I had to find out from God what the real message was. I had to make sure I was hearing Him. The Lord said to me" Automatic Grace is for fools, the closest people to me must have true repentance to me before any grace will be given" I trembled with fear and became scared to preach or teach. I the Archbishop could no longer perpetrate, or try to cover up what thus didn't say the Lord!

My God, I had compromised in order to seek and gain recognition from mankind. God commissioned me to love all people; He commissioned me to capture the remnant of God's people; He commissioned me to set the captives free; He commissioned me to reach all souls; He commissioned me to tell the truth regardless if it hurt or not; He commissioned me to speak what only the Lord said speak and no more; He commissioned me to uphold the blood stained banner regardless of what mankind said or did to me; He commissioned me to be a vessel in which He could use to bring people closer to His saving Grace. He commissioned me to introduce people to the only Savior, the Lord Jesus Christ. He commissioned me to take the heathen Gentiles, and show them that they too can be a part of the Body of Christ. He commissioned me to gather the outcast and assemble them to the four corners of the earth. He commissioned me to teach the Book of Life to those who can't read. He commissioned me to go to hell and back, in the Name of Jesus to reclaim the souls the enemy tried to hold on to. He commissioned me to a ministry that most ministers wouldn't even consider, because the job is too big and too dirty for the average Christian. He commissioned me to help transform lives all around the world to make an impact for Christ!

As a qualified Christian and Secular Counselor, I found myself in need of disposing of all those issues that kept me bound. I found myself doing what the world does. Again, *"Automatic Grace"* was not reality. The reality was that I still had baggage that needed to be dealt with. God was waiting for the opportunity to tell Satan; "Now you can intrude, but don't touch her soul." I fell for it! I was caught up in the hype of man's power. It was about me, me, and me. Hear me now…I didn't recognize the signs. I was traveling, doing what I love to do best, preach and teach. I operated in my own spiritual gifts. I was functioning in my own anointing. I was working my own prophetic-ness. Wrong! God said "Not so." The brakes hit quick, but I was still moving. I was bucking against the grain of the Holy Spirit. All the gifts the Spirit and apostolic and prophetic anointing of the living God poured into me was being done in vain.

The enemy had me, and I knew it; but I couldn't break free, because little did I know, this would become part of my story and true testimony for an appointed time. I understood why I was going through the storm. I couldn't back up, and was in too deep, but God did promise me that everything would become new. God's promises are true, and He is always faithful to His Word; *Revelation 19:11.*

You see, I was not blind to the downfalls in my life. I needed five (5) on it in order to speak the reality of my private hell and receive the permanent deliverance in my testimony; and permanent healing in my testimony. Coming out of bondage is in my testimony. Restoration of my Spiritual Renewal is in my testimony. Truth is in my testimony. I can't speak for others, but I sure speak for myself. I needed help as a Woman of God!

God dropped me in the boat to see if I trusted Him. I was on my own with a life jacket that contained everything the Lord had ever taught me. Everything my mentors had poured into me. Everything the prophet in my life (my biological father) had prophesied to me as a young girl. All that momma, and grandmothers and grandfathers had every shown me.

Those words were inside of this jacket and no one knew but me and God. The enemy knew because God released me to him. Satan knew that I was packing some powerful guns and he was trying to kill me with my own life jacket and gun.

"Automatic Grace", my brothers and sisters is not afforded to us, because just we're in ministry. There was spiritual surgery needed for my mind, body and soul. Yes I am a Woman of God, but if I say I am a Woman of the Church, then whose church do I belong too? Who is worthy enough to let me tell them my secrets of the past and present? The physical church and the folks in it is what hurt me. Not all physical churches are the same, but I do know from experience that the church is where I learned about "Automatic Grace" and a position. This is what I mislead me, and it cost me dearly. It costs to be anointed and I spilled it, and living by the Word of God. I failed!

Now visualize this scene…My life jacket is on and I'm ready to row across this long river of hell with Satan looking at me. He's real people because I saw him and recognized his darkness and capabilities. This was my fight with my stuff, and no invitations were given for this party! This was a private party that was going to be off the hook, and only the strong would survive. I had to let people know that it was nothing they could do for me, and then again, I was never asked could they do something for me. *The prayers of the righteous availeth much.…… there is non righteous, no not one!*

I had to remember who I was married to, and go back through the ceremony again in order to get it right, or let's just say I really needed to find out if indeed I went through a ceremony. We tend to forget where we come from and skip through some parts of the relationship with God, because we think we have all together. Well, sorry to bring you the report of the Lord, "if you haven't completed the ceremony, how do you expect to get His full Grace and Mercy?"

THE SHAKE DOWN (4)

O h! Why me. I don't want to live through this pain again. Can I get out of the boat Lord? Can somebody else row it for me? I'm tired. I am worn out. I am aching all over. My arms hurt. My legs hurt. My heart hurts. I have a headache, let me take some pills first and we'll pick this up later...I know that sounds familiar to somebody, because you know how we get when running from reality, and all we want to do is sleep so it will go away. This is what I said when I was only 2 strokes into the tribulation. I began to feel my body transforming, and I was caught up in visions from the past. It hit me like a ton of bricks. I felt my stomach turn with anxiety, my eyes now truly open to what the Lord had been showing me about my childhood and how Satan interfered with my life.

God said "look" and I did. He said you had a wonderful childhood, but you have forgotten some years of pain you were hiding for a long time. He said "I know you preach about it, but you need to see that it was not your fault. He said I needed you to remember the whole story. So I began to relive the molestation that took place when I eight (8) years old. I remembered the anguish, the shame, the filthiness and the violation I felt. I hid this for years until I had my first child. I forgave him right before I gave birth and told my mother. I have seen this perpetrator at all the reunions over the years and thought I forgave him. But I didn't! This floated up out of the water around the boat like a balloon. The pain associated with this memory had been suppressed, but I couldn't remember details. But just like the devil, he won't let you forget, and I began to remember, and the enemy began to laugh at me. There was nothing I could do, but watch.

Incest popped up like a cheap video. I had to relive this secret that had never been told. I had an older female cousin that I would go on trips with. I remembered on this one trip being in the bathroom with her. Because she was much older than me, she asked me to wash her private area. I didn't know any better, and was told not to tell. We laid on the floor side by side, and she told me how to wash her vagina. The lights were off; and then my aunt was called for us; my cousin answered for both of us, and she stated was finished. I remember getting up and turning the on, and telling my aunt that she was almost finish with washing me up. It was a lie! It was incest, and I was a victim of what was happening to her, and at some point in this sick act, it became consensual, and continued for a while. This too was a floating outside the boat like a balloon, and again the enemy laughed at me. At this point all I could do is watch the cheap video in disgust.

Flash…now I'm at church praising God. I'm watching the Apostle, Prophet, Evangelist, Pastor, Teacher, Ushers, Deacons, Mothers, Musicians, and Choir, and I remember wanting to be a part of it. Oh yea…. I'm being groomed for Five-Fold Ministry. I'm being shown how the church functions. I'm going to classes at an early age to get knowledge of what God requires of me. Wow! I see things going wrong! The devil said sarcastically "have you forgotten about being asked to come into the Pastors office and working side by side with him, he said you were the bomb?" I was so sickened by watching my attitude, and then watching this cheap video being played that no remote could stop. I couldn't believe it, was in love with Pastor and thought he was in love with me. I actually was getting paid money to sit on his lap. He told me that as long as I kept myself clean and fresh he would always pay me. I was able to go to special workshops and seminars. I got the best teaching, but little did I know that I was paying a price to be the bomb. The cheap video began to shake me down more, and things became intense. The enemy was laughing yet again. He said "Look what you've become, a whore for those high powered men and women who call themselves lovers of God." I was shown going to the conventions checking into a hotel suites and waiting for an envelope to be passed under my hotel door to give me an assignment for the new preacher that joined the big boys club. The wives of these men were on one floor and the calls girls on another. I saw myself being used to satisfy both wives and husbands in acts of sin that were going to following me. I never touched the women, they would always want me to just lay there and allow them to live out their fantasies. The enemy said "look at all that money you made; but don't forget to pay the pastor for helping you." The devil is a cold joker, Then the devil said "you were one hell of treat to those people you serviced." He was not letting up anytime soon…I think he was holding popcorn and soda as he shook me down again.

This particular float was large, but it was a different color. I was throwing up. I was not well. My soul was releasing issues I never truly dealt with in depth. I felt myself moving, but the floats were moving too. I found myself rowing trying to get away but a rope was around my neck. I had no idea at what point the rope was place upon me or where it came from. It wasn't the yoke of Christ! I began to see the drugs and alcohol and prison experiences flash by. The prison experiences weren't because I was an inmate; it was me sleeping with a correctional officer. I had to laugh at the devil. I told him you can't use that one, it's been dead for far too long. He said "watch this" and I said "You are only a nightmare," but it wasn't. It was my story! I saw my self in relationships that were so unhealthy and really wanted to know why. I mean how could I knowing Christ marry a man so much older than I, and be used as a toy? How did I compromise? Was it infatuation, was it really love? I was the only one of my friends hooked up. I had nice stuff, diamonds, gold, cars, limos, everything a young girl could only dream about, and I was living it as a well kept young woman of God. Here's the cost factor…I had to accept a beating everyday, whether it was physical, emotional, psychological, or through a twisted word of God; you name it, it was all for love, or so I thought. I said "God released me from that relationship, only after I was hospitalized with multiple facial and cranial contusions, my eye's beaten shut, and near a coma. The next relationships shown were really friendships and I never got too involved emotionally. Then the devil said "you were still involved in lewd acts of horror with so many men and women, I said "I was young and promiscuous, and was groomed for this kind of work. I couldn't believe the conditioning of mind, and how I was watching myself with this type of attitude and behavior. Along with this attitude came this dark shadow that covered the water and the boat. I was thrust with another rope around my neck and this time it was me being raped. I was being tortured. I saw their faces, and began to scream at the top of my lungs begging for it stop, and it did. I had covered it up for years. The hurt from this had dealt me a big blow in life and I became even more promiscuous, and it lead to legal prostitution. You were good the devil said. He said" when you were in the church you were doing God's work remember; he said" now your not in the church so this is how you had to survive" He laughed at me again; I got even more angry, but this is how the enemy shakes you down.

Now…this shake down was heavy, and all I wanted to do was take some pills again and go to sleep. Whew, domestic violence played a big part in my life, and I had seemed to find men that fit this description, you know nice on the outside with a camouflaged inside, and a sick mind. I subjected myself to this kind of behavior all my life, even in the church, and saw the marriages in the church struggle with this madness going on. It proved to be ineffective in my relationships. All these floats were in the water. Satan said "who are going to try and save now; you can't save yourself!" then ministry popped up. Oh man! I didn't want to see this. I thought I forgave everybody, but I had anger and animosity against any

17

and everybody. I now had to face the real horror of being gifted and in control of a great ministry and seminary that God groomed me for, and failed…so I thought!

I accepted my call to ministry and the current husband I had didn't quite get it. I was educated when he met me and continued to get my education. I was completing my Ph.D. and worked hard to take care of the kids. I was in an environment that didn't believe that Women were called to preach, and it blew me away to be convinced to believe this. I know what I was taught, because the Bible says *"And how shall they preach except they be sent? As it is written, HOW BEAUTIFUL ARE THE FEET OF THEM THAT PREACH THE GOSPEL OF PEACE, AND BRING GLAD TIDINGS OF THINGS! Romans 10:15*

And whosoever shall not receive you nor hear your words, when ye depart out of that house or city, shake off the dust of your feet. Matthew 10:14. I had to let the devil know that I never slept my way to a position. I earned every degree that I have. I let him know that the Lord has kept me and sustained me through hard times. I begin to tell him that I had to fight off your wolves that wanted to steal from me and borrow from me, and take advantage of me and the gifts that God has poured into me. I began to row and I felt the rope loosen up. He the (devil) was mad at me. I began to row some more, and flash…he put me in the middle of the hospital. I was wrapped up like a mummy. I had to remember the cancer. I testified of being healed and delivered from this disease, but he said, "But you never mourned the loss of your breast to cancer; you never mourned the loss of you reproductive organs to cancer; he said "you can't make any man happy because you can't have anymore children. He said you haven't cried yet" He said you always take the strong roll; he said you are nothing!" I became depressed in the boat, I got weak all over again, and he had shook me down. I tried to look through the darkness, but I couldn't see a thing.

My mental state was a blur and I felt like my life was over. All the floats were in the water so I thought. But, there was one more issue he had to shake me down with. The Spirit of Homosexuality. Oh no...Not me; don't go there. It's a sin! That's the biggest sin of all. I am an Archbishop. I hold the highest position that is known to the church world, and I'm a woman. I'll lose everything. God please don't allow me to see this one. Please don't let me fall into this temptation. I don't want to see this again. I thought we were done with this part of my life. Satan began to remind me of the first female relationship. It was violent and I was just there. But, God allowed the act to continue only as companionship. Then he reminded me of the second and I was dumped because I didn't know how to please her. I didn't have the physical connection to touch the same body parts that I have. I had no desire to learn either. I was reminded of all the homosexuality that runs rapid in my family. I mean I thought as a kid it was ok because everyone was with a man or a woman or both. I had aunts sleeping with nieces and vice versa for the men. I was also taught to love people in spite of what I thought. I was taught non-judgementalism, but part of me was still in that bathroom with my cousin. Needing that comfort, wanting to be loved, cuddled and affirmed. I was hurting and in pain from the church world at large. I had been approached by high powered women in ministry that wanted me to be their partner. I had been promised money if I would just consider it. Satan said "you have to explain to me, I know how you feel; he said remember I have a hit out on you and everything you thought you dealt with; I'm here to keep it real and I'm going to tear you down and use who I want to do it!" Satan said I will use the closest one to you; you're armor bearer." I mean it came so swift that I didn't even know what to think or do. I began to feel emotions that I didn't think existed. This one was in the boat with me. This was not a float. This giant was in my face.

Yes, the Archbishop fell victim to mental illness, but also to the darkness of another's agenda. I can't sit and write about how to abstain if

I never went through it. At least that is how I feel. I had grown up with some preconceived notions and even though I know what the Word of God say's, I was taught to love everyone and not to judge. I was moved on so quick in my time of weakness of a nervous breakdown, and before I knew it I was caught up, and at that time I didn't know why, because I lost my mind. I found myself indulging in a relationship based on companionship, because the one intimate experience made me feel like a rape victim all over again. I felt nasty as she touched me. I felt filthy, I felt convicted and then I heard God say in that instant of feeling convicted that "I needed to show you that you are not a product of your environment or experiences growing up," so there was no more sexual contact. I then thought I was just going to have a friend in my armorbearer and it would be cool. She would then learn about me, my family, spend more time at my house, share secrets, cover me before and after I preached, intercede for me, and learn from me. Instead I was the one learning how to be a lesbian without sexual contact as a real heterosexual woman married to a man. My spirit man was messed up. I mean I was in anguish. I can't say that the companionship didn't feel good in the beginning because it did. How many of us men and women of God have been through this? How many of us can honestly say we know how the emotional attachment creates a *"soul tie"*? And once that *soul tie* is connected it is all over for you, at least it was for me. My flesh began to crave that attention; meaning my flesh began to yearn for a touch (cuddling) from someone whom I thought was the closest one to me. I had forgotten about the Lord and my husband. I was on my own agenda; ahhh....but God had another plan. I would be used to find out about these types of relationships, and began to do a case study, and became an activist not so much for same-sex marriage, but for people having the right to love who they want to love. I found myself rubbing shoulders with the big league folks that believed in the cause. I was encouraged. I was supported. I saw the mighty so-called men and women of God in homosexual circles, and what I saw that blow your mind, but I wasn't there to blow a whistle at that point. I mean they had very large churches, and preach against the very act they are committing. I saw preachers with wives, but had boyfriends, I saw wives with husbands but had girlfriends. I saw musicians as lovers with the directors and choir members. I saw deacons and ushers, and mothers, elders, etc. in the church pretending to be saved and sanctified, in the mix, but judging everybody.

Oh, back to me! Well I tell you, I probably would have ended this friendship/relationship sooner, but because of the case study in which she was aware of. I needed more information in order to fully understand the spirit of homosexuality and why there is such a stronghold on those who participate. Now mind you I was married to a man, and she had a real relationship and marriage to a woman, and they had a real wedding, which I didn't find out until after the fact. Then man who called himself my spiritual father, who was an Apostle, had been parked outside her home for a few days she said. I said "He's been showing up to every event I've been preaching at. I said "He told me he was going to leave his wife and the ministry God had given, and the vision he had would work well with what God had given me, but I declined his advance. This Apostle then asked me if I was getting paid, I said "Yes, He then asked if they would pay him if he got involved, I said I'd have to get back to you." Now, as I stated earlier he had been showing up to my events, but now he was asking me for money; but I didn't ask him to travel the distance. He began to blackmail me. Satan said "here we go," and the boat started moving again, and it flashed to the meeting the Apostle called. I remembered him calling me about six times to make sure I was would be in attendance, and he kept calling to find out where I was in driving time. I was intentionally two (2) hours late, and he was intentionally two (2) hours late in starting the meeting. At this meeting a blow was delivered. This so-called Apostle and spiritual father called me out on the carpet and told everyone my story. He had just left from this woman's house, the day before and wished us well. He said he himself had struggles and understood, and agreed that if we had a press meeting that we both would be on the same side and restore relationships and marriage between one man and one woman. He said he was going to *Prayer Mountain* with his armor bearer for a few days and would get back to us. He asked if we lived together, I said No, and you know I'm married to a man; she and I never lived together or shared anything. He found that odd. I told the Apostle that I need my freedom and that God was going to bring a change real soon, that this is just a season, and that it was my story, testimony and case study, and He hugged me in agreement not to say anything. That hug made feel even dirtier than I did by being in the relationship with her! The meeting was awful; I could take it, but she and other couldn't. She wanted to beat him up and tell him that his wife was in a hotel room in our town with the woman she was in prison with, and that he was trying to cover it up from his church; she had an inside scoop that I didn't, but I did see them together, but didn't know his wife went MIA for a few days. I was the softer one (the femme) as they say, and she was a femme butch. I sat there with all dignity, character and integrity, but inside I was crying and hurt, not just for myself, but for the people that were there who were infected by this act of cruelty, and venom. There were people there that knew what was going on, and his attempt to extort money became his mission.

I mean come on, he was my spiritual father, and I thought why would he hurt me and others in this way? Anyway, it started the decline of the ministry, but it enhanced the presence of more same gender loving people. I kept the motto I had been taught. Loving everyone for whom and what they were. No discrimination at all. I felt that if I could reach them, I could begin to teach them. Well, "she" was not well and began to act strange. I began to distance myself and filed for dissolution of the Domestic Partnership which had only existed for three weeks, and was terminated before any strides were made with Marriage Equality, and the Get Engaged movement. I had to ask myself is this worth it? I was having meetings to impress the Equality people and then found out that the women and men were still married to their heterosexual spouses, but kept the relationships as husband wives for the sake of the kids, medical insurance, 401K's, retirement, and full benefits! It was more drama behind the scenes in the Marriage Equality/Equality California than one might think. If I was going to live a lie lifestyle I had to become an equal. I became an equal alright! I was asked to resign as the San Joaquin County Chapter Head because I got married to a man that I was already married to. Imagine that! It wasn't representative of what they EQCA/MECA wanted, but there were heterosexual couples that are chapter heads. I am keeping it real because most people wouldn't tell it, but I am!

So often this happens in ministry and we don't know how to get free. I had to get through this storm. I said well, we allow secular rappers to preach, R&B singers to preach and all the co-called worldly stuff in the church, maybe I'll be forgiven. Not so. I was an outcast. No prayer went forward. No one came to see me. I repented to God; I sought His face and ended up with a mess. In the newspaper, talk of the town, city, country and state. Then as if that wasn't enough; remember, I never lived with her, and she was married to a woman and shared homes. I was the one allowed to assess their relationship and help with the baby when they started acting up in public at the daycare and other places. The relationship was volatile between these two women. The one night I was greeted by with a knock on the door, and it was her pleading for us to get back together. I said "we were never really together, and you know what was going on, and that I thought you were happy with your wife; and that I have a husband," and declined her efforts. I said "my flesh crawls and my spirit is disrupted, I feel filthy and enough is enough." This was becoming violent as well…and pulled back to evaluate what I have done, and asked the Lord why me? A week later I had introduced her to my first love after 20 years of being apart. I'll say Becky instead of she….was angry and came to my home and threatened to kill me with a loaded firearm. I was going to die….She had a car full of kids, and went into the trunk to get more ammo. She tried to cross the threshold of my house and I laid her out with one blow. She got up and the kids wrestled her to the ground. She went back to the car and the kids yelled and said "mom she's going to shoot," and then sirens came, and she tried to hop a fence, but they caught her. We took the kids and waited for her family to arrive so the kids wouldn't go to child protective services. You know the rest; I'm still here by the grace of God. I have no one to blame, not even the devil, although it was his last shakedown, and he did that! I fell for it, hook line and sinker. My world, my children, the embarrassment, the shame, the hurt and no one to help, not even my new love.

NOT SO! (5)

Hey, hey...Not, so, I will live and not die....I'm yelling at this point and the boat is full of water, and I'm screaming "Devil you are a liar from the pit of hell!" I began to accept the fact that I had did all this stuff. I repented and ask God for forgiveness. Mankind had nothing to offer me but more pain and anguish. People were disassociating themselves from me, the rope, the boat, the water, the floats, everything began to drown me. I had no way out. Satan was killing me physically, and if he could do this, it would kill my soul and I would be in an eternal hell. I couldn't see or think, and then I began to hear *1 John 2:19; They went out from us, but they were not of us; for if they had been of us, they would no doubt have continued with us; but they went out, that they might be made manifest that they were not all of us vs. 20 But ye have an unction from the Holy One, and ye know all things. Vs 21 I have not written unto you because ye know not the truth, but because ye know it, and that no lie is of the truth. Vs22 Who is a liar but he that denieth that Jesus is the Christ? He is the antichrist, that denieth the Father and the Son. Vs23 Whosoever denieth the Son, the same hath not the Father: [but] he that acknowledgeth the Son hath the Father also. Vs 24 Let that therefore abide in you, which ye have heard from the beginning. If that which ye have heard from the beginning shall remain in you, ye also shall continue in the Son, and in the Father. Vs25 And this is the promise that he hath promised us, even eternal life. Vs26 These things have I written unto you concerning them that seduce you. Vs. 27 But the anointing which ye have received of him abideth in you, and ye need not that any man teach you: but as the same anointing teacheth you all things, and even as it hath taught you, ye shall abide. Vs. 28 And now, little children abide in him; that, when he shall appear, we may have confidence and not be ashamed before him at his coming. Vs 29 If ye know that he is righteous, ye know that everyone that doeth righteous is born of him.*

I wept and wept. I was sinking deeper and deeper. I could hear the scripture being recited to me as if it were a nursery rhyme. Satan's strategy was to kill me with my past, but God said "Not So" The Holy Spirit said "speak" I began to speak the law regarding the cleansing of the lepers and the consecration of the priest. I was getting ready to receive the blood and oil to my right ear, thumb and big toe. I was getting a two-fold anointing that was needed for my salvation. I am a believer and I am doing the work of the Word of God, I just got caught up…I needed a fresh anointing like David to begin to complete the task I was going to undertake for God.

I am worthy to have what God poured into me. Devil I am speaking to you right now! My life is too important to my Heavenly Father. Souls need to be saved. You forgot Devil I obtained an education in the name of My Lord and savior Jesus Christ. You have to submit to the authority that abides in me. I speak into existence the angels from on high that represent my army. I call on all the Apostles, Prophets, Evangelist Pastors and teachers who were before me to begin to summon me to the next level of my Lord. Devil in the name of Jesus you were allowed to get in my business, and I'm serving you notice that tonight your problem is even bigger now; you allowed me to see the past; I recognize it and guess what… I am healed, delivered and out of bondage. You can't keep me in this boat because I have to make to the other side of the veil where the people of God are hurting, and the women are sacrificing themselves, and classifying themselves as second class citizens, No so…..

So I said "I am giving you back this first rope you unqualified demon; I am issuing you a decree to never serve me another one like this; I am issuing you another decree to release the second rope in Jesus' mighty name; How dare you try to use a three foot cord without God's approval as a choke hold; you have been a perpetrator for years, but you met your match. God has brought me from a mighty long way. At this point I felt my help coming on, the Holy Spirit entered into this boat began lead me, and guided me to all understanding. I speak to every giant that ever entered into my life. *I have confessed my sins, he is faithful and just to forgive me of my sins and to cleanse me from all unrighteousness 1 John 1:9.*

I only speak for me and what I need as a mighty Woman of God. Lord I am getting above the water, and my arms are tired, but I must press to get the other side of the veil where I'll see the beauty and my blessing. The darkness that keeps us bound for years is not going to take control. The generational curses have stopped with me. I will not carry them any longer, it is not my stuff. I do take back all the enemy has stolen from me, but keep what doesn't matter, but give me my mind, give me my soul, give me my body, give me my education, give me my God given gifts back….I played with you for a little while but the time has come for you to be cast into a lake that contains your foul spirit. How many of us really speak to the enemy. We get scared to face him. He is nothing but a form of an astro-projection of our subconscious that increases with sin. I had to learn this the hard way. I played in his yard and tried to run out before he caught me. Satan was already waiting with keys to the gate, and to my flesh to keep it bound, but Not so say's the Lord! Proper etiquette and big profound words will woo you, but I need you to hear the truth men and women of God. Being in the boat is a tough ride, the rowing in strenuous, the water is cold; but the life jacket is the Word of God. He will bring all things to remembrance. I thank God for helping me, see me. I know Satan was allowed to enter in but he had to have permission first. I am that Proverbs

31 woman today. Today I choose my battles. I have prayed this prayer daily: *"And Jabez called on the God of Israel, saying, Oh that thou wouldest bless me indeed, and enlarge my coast, and that thine hand might be with me, and that thou wouldest keep me, from evil, that it may not grieve me! And God granted him that which he requested. 1 Chronicles 4:10.* We all prayed it, but some of us are still stuck in the boat without the necessary skills. I have to be diligent in my process to reclaim my dignity to represent God in the fashion in which He first intended for me to represent His agenda represented.

I now know the lesson that needed to be learned. The Holy Spirit ministered to me in such a way, that every time the water was in my throat I was able to fight back spiritually. I thought my spirit man was dead. I thought because of what others said that I was no longer a child of God. They were wrong; I am just as much of a Child of God as anyone. I am making it right by going through the necessary stages of turmoil in ministry and life. I am willing to face me at all times. I am willing to deal with me at all times. I am willing to put the people pleasing down. I am willing to get off any soapbox I may have been on placed by myself or others. I am willing to keep your commission to me Lord! So Devil I rebuke everything you stand for. I rebuke the sickness in my mind and my body you have tried to put on me all these years. I am not crazy. How dare try to make me lose my mind and give up all God has given me! You foul giant of misguided information. Yes I played in your field one too many times, but you messed up, you thought when you let me see me I was going to give up on God, Not so, I love my Heavenly Father more than I have ever loved Him before and I love me more than ever before. You tried to make me hate myself so I would destroy myself, but you are the one who has become the dirt that trods on the bottom, of the bottom of my shoes. Your tricks, your friends you sent me, your teachers and preachers you sent to me, were only the set up for the fall, But, *Greater is he that is me than he that is in the world.* I know longer need to seek out people to help with Gods work. He will send me who He wants to be a part of the ministry work needed to reach the remnant of His people. I have purpose. Once I said I have purpose the boat began to move faster. The more I was able to get free of all that was binding me the boat was moving at such rate I thought it had a motor on it. I saw the floats of my sins in the water blow up like sticks of dynamite were in them. I saw the emotions of the past sink to never return. The ropes were loose, my hands were sore my body was aching, but my soul was rejoicing. The sky was getting clear. There was a light shining that had to be reached, and then Satan surfaced again with the spirit of homosexuality, I told him to take it back to where it came from because it was no longer my story, and if he chose to be unfit it was on him but this day I choose whom I will serve and wasn't him, it was the Lord God almighty. I told him that I never was attracted to women; I said I never really dealt with women and how dare you put me in a trick bag. I had to talk to him as though we were on the street, I had to use my street IQ because he was trying to "pump fear" in me, I said "Not So," and I remembered the first scripture that had been given to me by a powerful Woman of God that was one of my mentors when I was growing up spiritually, she said read this every time you feel fear, "*vs.10 Fear thou not; for I am with thee: be not dismayed; for I am thy God: I will strengthen thee; yea, I will help thee; yea, I will uphold thee with the right hand of my righteousness. vs. 11 Behold, all they that were incensed against thee shall be ashamed and confounded: they shall be as nothing; and they that strive with thee shall perish.*

Isaiah 41:10, 11.

I remembered this scripture so clearly now and had to let the enemy know that you cannot use my situations any longer against me. I believe the prophecy of the great prophet Isaiah to Israel. I believed that I was having an Israel experience. I believe that because my temple is the Lords

I had stuff being sold out of it. I believe that the things in it weren't even mine. I began to realize that the redeemer of my soul had appeared. I believe that God was making provisions for me right there in the water. I began to see it as beautiful and abundant. I began to see how He provides for His own, and I was the Lords. He promised me rivers, fountains and springs of water. I believed that when the Lord said "Not So" He meant that in the supply of water He had given me, He would plant various trees in my wilderness. The Word of God became truly living water in boat. I know that the heathens were worshipping their own righteousness and were preying on me. They the heathens were trying to make a case against me with strong arguments of judgment. These heathens had no right to try and make me bow down before them when they themselves still haven't bowed to the Almighty Father. The heathens represented the friends, the ministry folks and spiritual parents. You know how it gets, they get what they need from you and kick you to the curb, and then try to predict your future and say it was by divine inspiration. God said "Not So" The Holy Spirit produces all that you need. The fulfillment of my destiny is linked to my direction I take from the Holy Spirit. "False prophecies have been given to you in my name said the Lord, you shall no longer concede to what man wants or feels you should do. There is no predictive prophecy my daughter for you…All past, future and present events will be given by divine inspiration, and the evidence will be that of the Holy Spirit". I began to praise God for whom He is!

The giant disappeared. The Word of God was to far deep in my soul to give up. I was to close to my destiny here on earth. The game had been played and now it was my last move. No more stuff was in the boat, not even other people's issues. I was close, I saw little trickles of things trying to hang on, but every time it tried to lash out to defeat me I began to praise the lord even more, I began to recite *"He that dwelleth in the secret place of the Most High shall abide under the shadow of the Almighty. I will say of the*

Lord, He is my refuge and my fortress: my God; in him will I trust. Surely he shall deliver thee from the snare of the fowler, and from the noisome pestilence. He shall cover thee with his feathers, and under his wings shalt thou trust: his truth shall be thy shield and buckler. Thou shalt not be afraid for the terror by night: nor for the arrow that flieth by day. Nor pestilence that walketh in darkness; nor for the destruction that wasteth at noonday. A thousand shall fall at thy side, and ten thousand at thy right hand; but it shall not come nigh thee. Only with thine eyes shalt thou behold and see the reward of the wicked. Because thou hast made the Lord, which is my refuge, even the Most High thy habitation. There shall no evil befall thee, neither shall any plague come nigh thy dwelling. For he shall give his angels charge over thee, to keep thee in all thy ways. They shall bear thee up in their hands, lest thou dash thy foot against a stone. Thou shalt tread upon the lion and adder: the younger lion and dragon shalt thou trample under feet. Because he hath set his love upon me, therefore will I deliver him: I will set him on high, because he hath known my name. He shall call upon me, and I will answer him, I will be with him in trouble; I will deliver him, and honor him. With long life will I satisfy him and show him my salvation"   *Psalm 91:1-16*

I became even surer that I was made by Christ himself. I became even more aware that I was covered and secure. I know I was being taken care of. I was under watch care with the Lord, and He was faithful in protecting me. I had to recall the deliverance, healing and be loosed in the name of Jesus! I realized that the deliverance had to be in God's will and that even when harm came my way, He still had me covered.

AGAPE LOVE (6)

Moments in time have gone by. I am tired and weary. I have made to the other side of the veil, and have been kept by His Spirit. I am drained and drenched with water sweat, tears, and shed some blood on the way over. I am stepping out of the boat without fear or apprehension. I am walking towards my destiny. I have fallen in love all over again. I see my blessings right there…the manifestation is coming and I can feel it in my soul. I am excited, and the Fruits of the Spirit are popping out all over the place. My tree is full of fresh fruit. A fresh anointing is always what God requires of me to have and I must press to get to the spring that awaits my arrival.

On the wall of the rocks it says: *"Remember ye not the former things, neither consider the things of old. Isaiah 43:18.* It was real…. I entered the water and it smelt like fresh flowers as my senses were aware. When I finished my shower I saw him, whom I had prayed for. It wasn't the other fly by night relationships when we think we're love, and get married, and find out he or she is a monster sent strait from hell, and hard to get rid of. I mean this was my first love. Granted I was already married to him, but I saw "him" that was looking for what I thought he said was his rib. I wept, but didn't disregard the fact that it could have been a trick. Guess what, it was. I made so many mistakes, and we divorced, and reconciled because the pastor said it was the right thing to do, but God didn't tell me to do it. I trusted again, but God released me from that marriage only after He showed me how evil and cruel he was. He became involved in pornography, and talking to people that were not in our home about getting Palimony? he became perverted and eventually acted out his perversions; he began dosing me with my psych medication Effexor until the Lord gave me a flash of a bottle under my bathroom sink. I sat there for a moment, and went to cabinet and found the substance. I retained a portion for testing, and poured out the rest; and since there no longer was any Effexor, he distanced himself, and began to get clarity of my thoughts and emotions, and my capacity to love diminished; and my respect for him disappeared, and went into complete survivor mode in order to protect the kids and me. This was someone who knew the good the bad the ugly of my life growing up, and I he. This was someone who has been through a few storms and had nothing to lose either. This was a man seeking God's face and willing to do whatever the Lord asked him to do. We are all not perfect, but it's a blessing when you know he came from God (or so we think). All the counseling I had done could not compare to what was going on in this reality of being exposed to the manifestation of "Agape Love" I know we speak about it. I know we pray for the presence of the Lord to be bestowed upon us with this great love that seems to be inevitable with us here on earth. I was released to this man, and he was released to me after 20 years. God restored us back to each other and prepared us for each other. It was real, oh so real. I mean how many of us out there marry people, and are still in love with someone else. How many men and women get into a relationship and it is only for what it looks like to others in ministry? In speaking for myself, but if anyone feels the same way say AMEN for the truth! Keeping it real and telling my story and testimony is a reality for me in this tenth (10th) season of my life. I kept it real before, but wouldn't let anyone else in my house (my person). I am now ready to keep it real and share my reality with someone who has nothing to gain or lose from my openness. Our, my reality is the faith that serves the same God. "We" worship Him in spirit and in truth. We follow the Ephesians 5 rule of thumb and yet we have our individuality that is oh so beautiful.

Today I am alert and aware. I walk in the Spirit of the living God and remain teachable. I was never unruly, but a little outspoken and head strong. I have leaned to hear others and truly listen to what there are saying without reading the conversation, and because I don't have time for a read between the lines lifestyle.

Yes I was a wretch with no grace or mercy, and now because the Lord has saw fit to Heal, Deliver and loose me from bondage, and come clean with myself, I have been given complete authority to walk talk in the assurance of signs and wonders following me...healing miracles and atmosphere's set for my gifts, but being the vessel that God uses to manifest His power and not mine. I am no longer broken in thousands of pieces by the hands of man, and have been given a new beginning and a new birth. The theology and philosophy of all my educational background will only be important to those that really want to know me or tear me down, but men and women of God legitimacy is what I bring on this journey to the other side of the veil. The degrees don't make my soul, but the journey and my belief in Christ does. The credentials are what make me qualified in the eyes of man to walk through doors and obtain what is rightfully mine as a child of God. I earned the education to help build the body of Christ, to help equip and train the men and women of God for the effective work of the ministry of Jesus Christ and to win lost souls to Christ. I cannot properly market the Word of God if I don't know it. I believe that because I have found out what God really requires of me, it will allow Him to market me to a lost and dying world of Saints and Aint's that really don't know Him.

The Remnant is who the Lord is restoring to build the Kingdom of God, so don't miss it! You must have "Agape Love" in order to be effective and not selective in ministry, or selective in whom you have sitting in your pews and pulpits. We, together as brothers and sisters in Christ have to know what we're searching for, and know what we are looking for in order for healing and deliverance to take place in our services corporately, and individually, and offer freedom to all who come in contact with us.

My journey to the other side of the veil is a deep one that continues daily with supplication anywhere I stand and sit. It may be in song, it may be in prayer, it may be via the atmosphere, or via a trance…..I have gotten there, so come and go with me….

The Other Side of the Veil (7)

My God, my God, My God......the other side of the veil looks just like the Throne Room. God said in his word that He would speak to me directly in this season of my life. God said that the prophecy over my life has now been opened to the realm in which He needs me to walk in. I now see the elements of my testimony as a revelation to greater spiritual insight, power and anointing. I see the beauty of regeneration of the soul. I understand the transitions of glory to glory. I see the acclimation of my soul as I transform into the light that walks in an anointing that can only be obtained through the purity of one's heart and life. I feel the presence of God ever so present throughout my daily life, and am able to tap into God's source without a whole lot of fanfare and pomp and circumstance. This is so awesome, this is so powerful, this is so beautiful, this is so fulfilling to my soul to know that I sat for over ten (10) years while the Lord did a work in me for His good, and for my good. I have been able to embrace the call on my life and recognize the warning signs and triggers that would try to make me repeat the past mistakes. God has called me into the light of His Holiness in order to feel the passion behind the mission, purpose and destiny for my life. The Deity of Christ Jesus The Prophet, In His incarnation fulfills a three-fold ministry. That of a Prophet, a Priest and a King. On the other side of the veil is where I was able to take a look at His ministry as a Prophet, it was foretold in *Deuteronomy 18:15*, "The Lord thy God will raise up unto thee a Prophet from the midst of thee, of thy brethren, like unto me; unto ye shall hearken." As a Prophet He brought light, knowledge, understanding from sin's darkness and established His kingdom of grace and truth. He began His Prophetic ministry to people under the Law and sent His disciples out to these people saying, "Go not into the way of the Gentiles, and into any City of Samaritans enter ye not. But go rather to the lost sheep of the house of Israel." *Matthew 10:5,6*. After His rejection, however, He sends them out again as recorded in *Matthew 28:19*, "Go ye therefore and teach all nations.." They were sent out first to the Jews to preach the Kingdom. After His rejection they were again sent out to all the world to make disciples.

I was the woman rejected over ten (10) years ago only to be the example of Jesus' spoken words of truth in Scripture.....I see and identify with the example of Jesus with the Syrophenician Woman who came to Jesus to ask Him to cast forth the devil out of her daughter. "But Jesus said unto her, let the children first be filled; for it is not meant to take the children's bread, and to cast it unto the dogs. And she answered and said unto Him, "Yes, Lord: yet the dogs under the table eat of the children's crumbs." *Mark 7:27, 28*. As recorded in *Matthew 15:22. 23*. This woman approached Him saying, "O Lord thou Son of David...But He answered her not a word." Then she said, "Lord help me." This is a beautiful passage as it shows that the Messiah to the Jew is also the Savior to the Gentile. This woman, a Gentile, appeals to Him as the Son of David. He answers her not a word. Then she worshipped Him saying, "Lord help me." The Lord listens to her as the Lord, not as the Son of David. The Lord He heard me.....

"He taught that His Kingdom is something new and distinctive; that it is more spiritual, and not political; that it is invisible and internal; that it is silent, mysterious, and progressive; that it is universal in its design and scope. That it is social; that by it we enter into a relation, not only to God, but also to men; that it can be entered only by regeneration; and that it is both present and future," while the characteristics of a Prophet are Divinely Commissioned and evident in the case of Jesus by many Scriptures attesting the fact and mentioned in the following as such: (1) At His baptism. *Mark 1:9-11.* (2) Sent to do the Father's will. *John 4:34.* (3) The work of the Father. *John 5:17.* (4) The Father hath sent me. *John 5:30.* (5) His works were of the Father. *John 10:32.* (6) Finished the work He was given to do. *John 27:4.* His final work, that of the cross, was preceded by a time of preparation, a time of special anointing which took place on the Mount of Transfiguration, so He must be gifted! Jesus was gifted in preaching, teaching and healing! Jesus was preaching and proclaiming our God to the multitudes, Jesus was teaching and expounding the gospel to the disciples, Jesus was healing and illustrating the gospel to the sick!

I entered into the journey of being in the throne room where the veil was, and I am now walking towards the right side of the veil ready to walk into full purpose and destiny. As I got ready to turn the corner the Scriptures illuminated like a rolodex in my mind, body and soul. The words were clear and concise the Scriptures read Revelation 4:6 "And *before the throne there was a sea of glass like unto crystal: and in the midst of the throne, and round about the throne, were four beasts full of eyes before and behind."* Then I saw *Revelation 15:2* and it *read "And I saw as it were a sea of glass mingled with fire, and them that had gotten the victory over the beast, and over the image, and over his mark, and over the number of his name, stand on the sea of glass, having the harps of God."* I sang as I was being led to the other side of the veil as the transparency of the stones held me captive as lenses of crystal, and all I could see was yet another Scripture and it read *Revelation 21:18 "And the building of the wall of it was of jasper and the city was pure gold, like unto clear glass."* I found myself in a Time Warp and the Across Stick appeared as thankfulness, innocence, mercy, evangels, witness, awesomeness, reconciliation and peace. My dreams became a reality and visions with foresight and prophecy knowing where I came from and moving forward with promise of greater things to come. I knew that life was about learning to cope, living, and staying focused and true to thine own purpose of joy and happiness, and that the gems stones represented each level I would achieve once I reached the other side of the veil. God had found me spotless and without sin. God had now found me trustworthy to walk in the spiritual gifts once again as an Apostle and Major Prophet to speak what saith the Lord whether I got paid or not, but to remain in constant relationship regardless of what the atmosphere and others were doing. The glass, oh the glass would now represent the purity of my heart and treasures that lay within my being.

Stay with me as we travail together through the glass, the crystal the awesome and magnificent aroma was over powering as I became emotional at the sight of the angels worshiping, and then my soul began to magnify the Lord with tongues I've never been able to interpret until now. I felt my womb fill with His glory, fill with His gifts, fill with His fruits, fill with His Middle Voice that would be Esoptron of rendered glass as I collected its ambiance as a an abstract of divine presence. Ahh…I understand the hyalinos of the glassiness of the sea and why it beckons and calls to me to be present and accounted for during worship and devotion unto Him, the King of Kings and the Lord of Lords. I now understand why those emblems of thalassa have to be fixed in purity. I was that vessel He needed to refine in order to carry out this mandate and Word from on high, and that all that appertains to the authority and judicial dealings of God would become my mantle as the breaking of the noisy surf roared like a lion.

Lord you have brought me to this place in you to be used like ice, and be congealed and transparent as the krystallos of a precious stone, and raised up to be like rock crystal which is pure quartz that crystallizes as an hexagonal prism with each pyramidical apex I reach on the other side of the veil. I have become brightness and transparency to shine like crystal as in *Revelation 21:11 "Having the glory of God: and her light was like unto a stone most precious, even like a jasper stone, clear as crystal."* Yes Lord….I understand that the ministry in me is pure and cannot be tainted by the world, so I became pregnant with Crystal Rain and Treasures of the Heart. There is nothing or no one that can cause me to stray away from that which I have seen, and become in the Lord. This was a mission that even I couldn't mess up, because God' won't allow me to get attached to things, people, or organizations that may resemble anything less than His appearance and manifestations. I now have to function as transitive force in order to transform into crystal, and the splendor as of the effect of Christ upon and unto His saints. I know what the mirror reflects, and that goodness is what keeps me captivated in the presence of God. I see sheer panels of color in the throne room. I feel the fabric rubbing up against my soul and with every brush there was a stone dropped into my mind. I started worshiping into higher state of being which moved to me to the next level on the other side of the veil. The water was flowing with the natural essence of fragrances that stemmed from lotus flowers that had been blossomed and made their way into the throne room. I see the walkway with my name on it with instructions as Scriptures leading the way. I heard the middle voice say "your journey will continue as word of God is absorbed into my soul, and when I teach the words will always be illuminated, but only to you." I was overwhelmed with joy as the anointing was bathing me with every step. I hear *James 1:23 'For if any be a hearer of the word, and not a doer, he is like unto a man beholding his natural face in a glass,"* and then I heard *1 Corinthians 13:12 "For now we see through a glass, darkly: but then face to face: now I know in part: but then shall I know even as also I am known."* This was for me to understand the riddle's within the Scripture's given to me for growth during the divine revelations for my life, so others couldn't perpetrate my path, and the explosion of my ministry that would take effect in a differ time and space as mirror to the soul and eye's of the Lord.

The middle voice kept sounding off as I was on the glassy path and I saw the Scripture in parts and now I am able to piece them together as a way of standards for the ministry God was birthing inside me as a an immaculate conception. *1 Corinthian 3:18* was what God needed me to focus on as I would come in contact with more people that were addicted and afflicted in the church. *"Let no man deceive himself. If any man among you seemeth to be wise in this world, let him become a fool that he may be wise."* So the middle voice is the warning voice for me along this journey while on the other side of the veil. I see that being on the other side is where many will never reach in Christendom because their mandate and mantle is not the same as mine, but Jesus Christ is the only foundation we should have in common. If any man has a foundation build on his own, I am to flee and never return or associate with. I haven't always paid attention to the warning signs, but now I get it. Now I see it. Now I feel the wrong in my spirit man, and I become sensitive to the Spirit of God and recognize the spirits in actions, and God activates me to move by His power to tear it down in the supernatural before it manifests on earth. I thank God for giving me the insight and discernment to recognize and strike the enemies plot to destroy others and me.

I'm now approaching a white veil flowing like the waves in the sea. I am recognizing the sea of glass getting clearer and clearer. Men and women of God this was divine and caused me to have a picture forever etched in my mind. I am able to tap into God's power immediately when praying for myself or others; while teaching; while preaching; and while just talking about His goodness and mercy. God gave me the victory over the beast because I had faith. Yes, yes the victory is won because of your faith in Christ and refusal to submit to the Antichrist.

Being before God's throne is a victory no one could ever take away me. I am pure, I am Holy, I am righteous, I am able to enter into the temple as a servant of the most high, with my past no longer binding me, no longer haunting me; I can enter the temple with my mind stable and stayed on Jesus Christ, and knowing that I received the knowledge needed to succeed in the reconciliation, recovery, regeneration, restoration and refining as a Woman of God. I know stand on the concepts and principle's set before me, and have applied them to my life as mother, friend, pastor, teacher, Apostle, Major Prophet and Bishop in the Lord's Church. I stay humbly submitted to the headship and leadership in my life, and maintain accountability by being in authority, but not usurping authority.

My soul has been opened up. My mind, body and soul is in exploration of His mission, and evangelistic service to the world before they knew it would change the way we worship and adore Him who died for our sins. I realize the suffering I went through only prepared me for what I was going to see next. I am worthy to eat more than the crumbs from the table. I am gifted and anointed to obtain that portion which is mine as declared and decreed in Scripture, as the proclamations of the LORD are herald through me as voice of redemption to the people. I get it…Jesus is an unchangeable bill to never be exchanged for man's purposes.

My journey to the other side of the veil is a never ending story and testimony of God grace and mercy in and over my life. I will continue to praise and worship in the name of Jesus. I will continue to seek His face regardless of the situation. I receive the missing piece to the puzzle as LOVE truly sent from God. I will listen to the middle voice as I stay on The Other Side Of The Veil…

Printed in the United States
By Bookmasters

The Other Side Of The Veil is testimony, law of responsibility and journey of a woman that struggled with mental illness, addictions, afflictions, sin, and unresolved issues from the past that kept her bound to the same mistakes; But she is able to capture the essence of God's presence in her life and emerges into and through her 10th season as a restored, recovered, reconciled and refined Woman of God ready to receive the blessings of the LORD with the purity of her praise, worship, devotion and heart.

VerShay "DominaRex" DuVall is a Renown Christian Counselor. Her Concentrations, and fields of Specializations are: Christian Sex Therapy, Christian Marriage and Family Therapy, Christians and Chronic Mental Disorders, Christians and Drug/Alcohol Recovery, Christians and Domestic Violence, Christian Survivors and Victims of Rape and Molestation, and Tactical Military Initiative Divisional Counseling. She is a prolific and profound Evangelist, Christian Educator, Philosopher, Keynote and Inspirational Conference Speaker; Teacher, Preacher, Author, Actress, Life Coach, Spiritual Midwife, Live Radio Host, Entrepreneur, Philanthropist and Instructor for the International Sunday School Department of the Church of God In Christ. VerShay "DominaRex" DuVall is also an advisor to a host of Ministry Leaders and Corporate Business Executives around the world.

She is an Ordained Evangelist Missionary, Confirmed Apostle & Major Prophet given to the Body of Christ to preach and operate in the Spirit under a strong prophetic governing mantle that transcends racial, denominational and cultural barriers. She is known by an intense, but sweet, apostolic ministry of healing, deliverance, recovery, and establishing order as a Five-Fold Ministry Leader to the nations. It is her desire to be an effective servant in the Kingdom of God and to influence the lives of people in a positive way through the power of the gospel, and of the Holy Spirit. Her powerful evangelistic outreach ministry, experiences and testimony allows her to counsel men, women and children, and teaches them how to apply the storms of life as lessons through Biblical principle, concept and application.

VerShay "DominaRex" DuVall is a three (3) time Cancer Survivor, Birth Mother of 3, and Adoptive Mother of 2. She resides in Fayetteville, NC.

 authorHOUSE®

ISBN 978-1-4969-7476-1
51195

9 781496 974761

How to Go Through

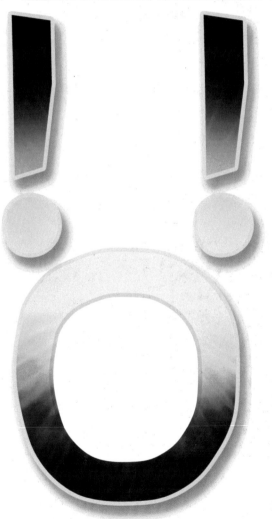

HELL

A fictional tale by the author of "Blessed with Bipolar"

R i c h a r d   J a r z y n k a